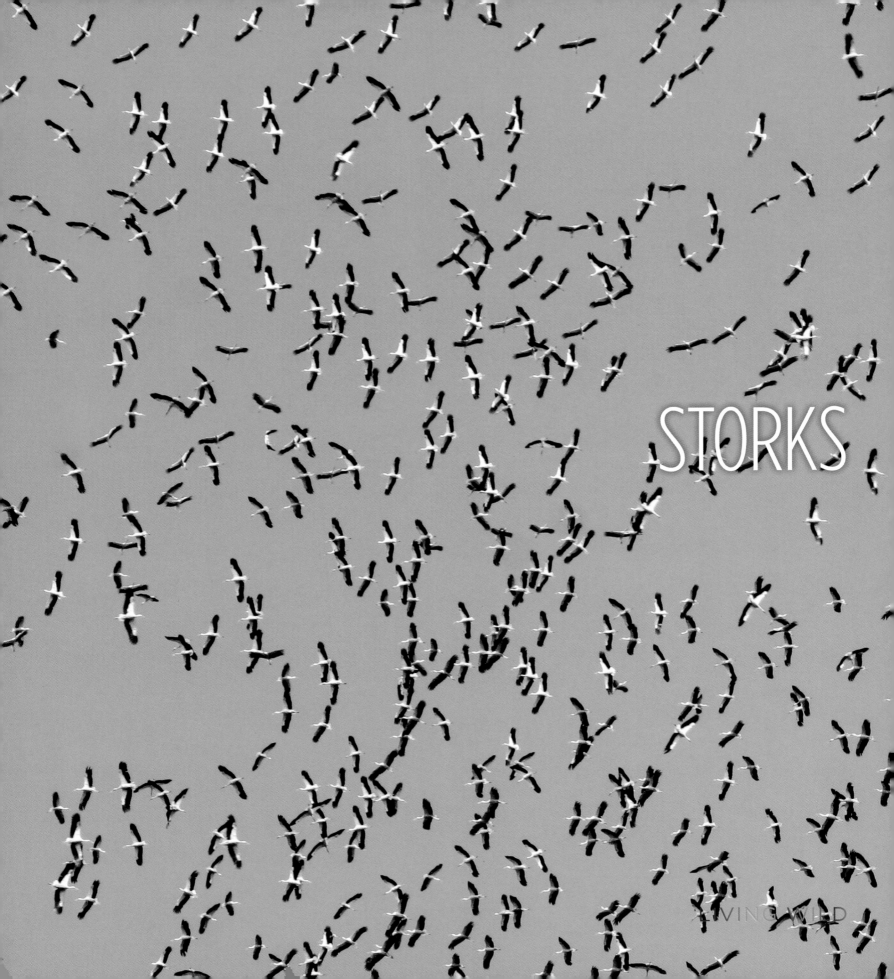

STORKS

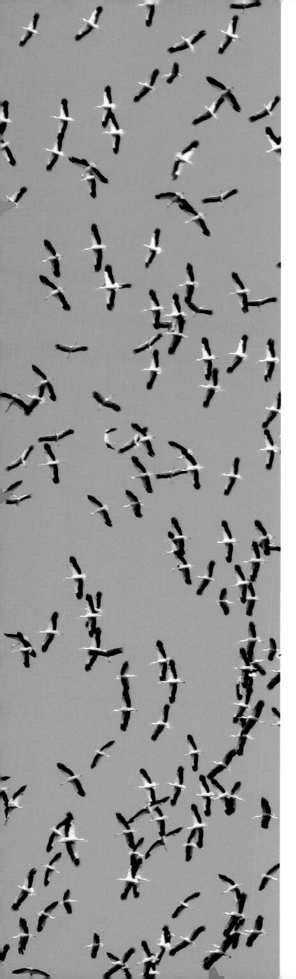

LIVING WILD

Published by Creative Education and Creative Paperbacks
P.O. Box 227, Mankato, Minnesota 56002
Creative Education and Creative Paperbacks are imprints of The Creative Company
www.thecreativecompany.us

Design and production by Mary Herrmann
Art direction by Rita Marshall
Printed in Malaysia

Photographs by Alamy (FLPA), Corbis (Johan Hammar/Naturbild, Martin Harvey, jspix/
imagebroker, Preau Louis-Marie/Hemis, John Lund/Blend Images, Steven David Miller/
Nature Picture Library, Richard Nebesky/Robert Harding World Imagery, Wild Wonders
of Europe/Máté/Nature Picture Library, Yoshitsugu Nishigaki/Aflo, Yue Yuewei/Xinhua
Press), Creative Commons Wikimedia (Paul Bransom, cuatrok77, Didier Descouens,
GDW.45, Dave & Margie Hill/Kleerup, Merlin, SandyCole, Einsamer Schütze, Andreas
Trepte, Rupal Vaidya), Dreamstime (Bddigitalimages, Lukas Blazek), iStockphoto (Ihar
Byshniou, EcoVentures-Travel), Shutterstock (360b, dean bertoncelj, Bildagentur Zoonar
GmbH, Volodymyr Burdiak, dan??o?lu, EBFoto, Erni, feathercollector, Sergey Kamshylin,
Ivan Karpov, Kenneth Keifer, kobps2, Leighton Photography & Imaging, francesco de
marco, np, Roberto Tetsuo Okamura, photoff, ScratchArt, Worakit Sirijinda, Dr Ajay
Kumar Singh, Andre Valadao, YANGCHAO, Zyankarlo)

Library of Congress Cataloging-in-Publication Data
Gish, Melissa.
Storks / Melissa Gish.
p. cm. — (Living wild)
Includes bibliographical references and index.
Summary: A look at storks, including their habitats, physical characteristics such as their long
legs, behaviors, relationships with humans, and their threatened status in the world today.
ISBN 978-1-60818-571-9 (hardcover)
ISBN 978-1-62832-172-2 (pbk)
1. Storks—Juvenile literature. 2. Rare birds—Juvenile literature. I. Title.

QL696.C535G57 2015
598.3'4—dc23   2014028013

CCSS: RI.5.1, 2, 3, 8; RST.6-8.1, 2, 5, 6, 8; RH.6-8.3, 4, 5, 6, 7, 8

First Edition HC 9 8 7 6 5 4 3 2 1
First Edition PBK 9 8 7 6 5 4 3 2 1

CREATIVE EDUCATION • CREATIVE PAPERBACKS

STORKS

Melissa Gish

It is late winter in Florida's Big Cypress National
    Preserve, and a patch of sawgrass marsh has begun to

dry up, trapping small fish in the muddy water. A flock of wood storks flies overhead.

It is late winter in Florida's Big Cypress National Preserve, and a patch of sawgrass marsh has begun to dry up, trapping small fish in the muddy water. A flock of wood storks flies overhead. They spot the small depression and, like a troupe of dancers in perfect unison, gracefully glide earthward. Their outstretched feet touch down and settle into the muck. Instantly, dozens of golden topminnows and mosquitofish splash wildly, but escape is impossible. The wood storks clack their bills, communicating their excitement. Then the feast begins, and within minutes, all the fish are gone. Bellies full, the storks rest, rubbing their bills against their breast feathers. Suddenly, the sawgrass shakes, and the storks feel the ground shudder beneath their feet. They flap their wings furiously and rise up in a flurry of white feathers—just in time to avoid the jaws of a hungry alligator.

WHERE IN THE WORLD THEY LIVE

■ **White Stork**
Europe, Middle East, southwest Asia, north-western and sub-Saharan Africa

■ **Black Stork**
Central Europe, Asia, and southern Africa

■ **Wood Stork**
southern United States to Argentina

■ **Asian Openbill Stork**
India and Sri Lanka

■ **African Openbill Stork**
sub-Saharan Africa

■ **Marabou Stork**
Africa

■ **Jabiru Stork**
Central and South America

■ **Black-necked Stork**
Asia and Australia

The 19 stork species live in a variety of habitats around the world, including forests, savannas, marshes, and wetlands. Their populations range from numerous to endangered. Species such as the white stork migrate annually from northern climes to southern feeding grounds. The colored squares represent areas in which eight stork species are found today.

WONDERFUL WADERS

Storks are found on every continent except Antarctica. The name "stork" is likely derived from the Proto-Germanic *sturkaz* (from an earlier language's word describing the stiff or rigid posture of the bird). People who spoke that language lived in northern Europe, where the white stork was abundant—and continues to live. Most other stork species prefer tropical regions. The 19 stork species belong to the Ciconiidae family in the order Ciconiiformes, named for the Latin *ciconia*, meaning "stork." Many other wading birds, including ibises, herons, egrets, and spoonbills were once grouped with storks, but **DNA** research has determined that these birds are not as closely related to storks as previously thought. Storks are characterized as having long legs and bills, and they fly more by gliding than by active wing-flapping. Though some species prefer drier habitats, most storks frequent marshes, ponds, and streams.

Six stork species are limited to Asian habitats. They are the milky, Storm's, and greater adjutant (all of which are endangered), as well as the painted, lesser adjutant, and Asian openbill storks. The black-necked stork is found

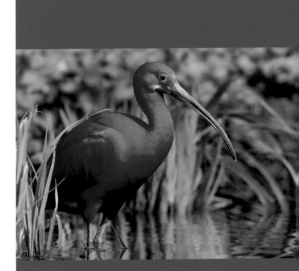

The scarlet ibis is commonly found in the warmest parts of South America and on Caribbean islands.

Storks migrating between northern Europe and South Africa may travel more than 12,400 miles (19,956 km) round trip.

The oriental stork can grow to nearly five feet (1.5 m) tall with a wingspan of more than seven feet (2.1 m).

in Asia and Australia. The maguari stork and jabiru are found only in parts of Mexico and South America and on neighboring islands. North America's lone stork species is the wood stork, which also lives in South America and the Caribbean. The endangered oriental stork once extended from Russia to Korea but is now found only in parts of Russia and China. Five species are found only in Africa. They are the yellow-billed, Abdim's, saddle-billed, marabou, and African openbill storks. The woolly-necked stork can be found from West Africa all the way across Asia to Indonesia. Two stork species that spend summers in Europe and then migrate to Africa for the winter are the white and black storks. Black storks are also found in far-southern parts of South Africa year round.

As birds, storks are **warm-blooded**, feathered, beaked animals that walk on two feet and lay eggs. All storks are large birds. The smallest stork is the Abdim's stork, also known as the white-bellied stork, which stands up to 29 inches (73.7 cm) tall and weighs about 2 pounds (0.9 kg). The largest stork species, the marabou stork, stands about 5 feet (1.5 m) tall and weighs up to 20 pounds (9.1 kg). Its average wingspan of nearly 11 feet (3.4 m) is one of

The Abdim's stork was named for Bey El-Arnaut Abdim, a 19th-century government official in Sudan.

Averaging heights of 5 feet (1.5 m), male saddle-billed storks are likely the tallest storks in the world.

the largest of any birds'. Storks' feathers, called plumage, range in color from white to gray to black. Many species have plumage in varying patterns that include **iridescent** black feathers. The painted stork has pink and orange markings, while Abdim's stork has blue markings on its face. Storks' bills may have color variations and patterns in black, yellow, and red.

Most storks eat frogs, fish, insects, and worms. Some species are scavengers, eating the flesh of dead animals. These storks have pink or reddish bare skin on their heads and necks, which helps them avoid getting mud and blood stuck to feathers. A stork's bill is made of keratin, the same material found in human fingernails. Bill shape is related to the foods storks eat. Scavenger storks have large, thick, sharp-edged bills for tearing meat from a carcass. Wood storks and other stork species that wade through murky water have bills that are sensitive to touch, snapping shut to trap prey that brushes against them. Other North and South American storks typically hunt in clear water, using their long, spear-shaped bills to skewer frogs and fish that they can see. These storks even hunt snakes and other small

The endangered greater adjutant stork breeds only in isolated areas of Cambodia and northeastern India.

Female saddle-billed storks have yellow eyes; males have brown eyes and small, yellow wattles that hang from the throat.

The "structural coloration" evident in black storks is caused by light interacting with the layers of the bird's feathers.

The black-necked stork is sometimes called "jabiru" in Australia, but the true jabiru is native to the Americas.

reptiles—including baby alligators. The Asian openbill stork has a specialized bill for eating mollusks, its primary food source. The stork's upper mandible (jaw) holds a snail, clam, or mussel to the ground, while its lower mandible slices the animal loose from its shell. Then the meaty prey is pulled out and consumed.

Storks have powerful eyesight. They can detect movement of prey and react instantly. The eye of a stork has a nictitating (*NIK-tih-tayt-ing*) membrane (a see-through inner eyelid) that closes from front to back, wiping dust from the eyeball and protecting it from struggling prey. It also shields the sensitive **pupil** from direct sunlight. Storks communicate with grunts and hisses because they lack an avian syrinx, the organ in birds that produces sound. They also clack the upper and lower parts of their bills together. This clattering may be combined with head bobbing and the spreading of wings to communicate anything from aggression toward intruders to interest in mating.

Storks have long legs that allow them to wade through deep water or tall marsh grasses without getting their bodies wet. The legs bend at the knee as the stork steps

Young Asian openbill storks lack the adults' characteristic gap between the upper and lower mandibles.

In 2013, British researchers began studying why fewer European storks have migrated to Africa in recent winters.

up, and its slightly webbed toes come together. As the stork steps down, the toes spread out, distributing the stork's weight so the bird does not sink into mud or wet sand. Like many birds, storks are anisodactylous (*an-EYE-suh-DAC-til-us*), which means they have three toes that point forward and one that points backward.

Like their ancestors, modern birds have hollow bones, making them lightweight for flight. Storks have powerful wings that are long and wide, which enables them to glide for great distances without pumping their wings. In open spaces, particularly in Africa, storks ride upward currents of warm air. These circular currents are called thermals. By riding thermals, storks can soar for hours without once flapping their wings and are thus often seen circling rather than soaring in a straight line. Storks also ride global air currents that help them migrate long distances annually. A 2003 study conducted by biologists at Tel Aviv University in Israel found that white storks migrating between Europe and Africa were able to travel much faster going south than going north because the air currents moving southward provided the birds with a tailwind, pushing them along.

Marabou storks are also called undertaker birds because of their long, black coat of feathers and nearly bald head.

White storks typically court and breed in continental Europe before migrating back to southern Europe and Africa.

RAISING A RUCKUS

Storks reach maturity and are ready to mate at three to four years of age. Storks practice serial monogamy. This means that once a pair of storks decides to mate, they build a nest together and remain paired for the duration of a breeding season. Then they spend the rest of the year alone or with other storks and return to their nest site each breeding season. The storks form an attachment to the nest site, not to each other. If one male gets chased away from a nest by a different male, the female will remain with the nest and mate with the new partner.

Breeding seasons vary by geography and are closely tied to seasonal food supplies. Tropical storks breed in the rainy season, when insects and caterpillars are plentiful. Storks such as the marabou, found on the African savanna, breed in the dry season, when shrinking watering holes lead to the deaths of weaker animals, which become the marabou's **carrion** meals. European white storks and wood storks of the Americas arrive at their breeding grounds in March or April so that their young can feed on the fish, frogs, and insects that are most abundant in summer.

Young painted storks eventually move far away from their parents, but as adults, they travel very little.

Several thousand migrating white storks are shot in Syria and Lebanon each year, because the birds are considered pests.

Nesting openbill storks make their home in India's Uppalapadu Bird Sanctuary, along with other migratory species.

Males arrive at the breeding grounds several days before females. They spend this time repairing and reinforcing the nest from the previous year. When females arrive, they assist in preparing the nest. Normally, storks create nests atop trees or high structures such as telephone or electrical poles, rooftops, and chimneys, though sometimes they nest among rocks or even on the ground. Stork nests are made of sticks and twigs, and the inside is filled with moss, turf, and other soft material. Storks add to their nests each year, making them bigger and deeper. Nests can be up to six feet (1.8 m) wide and nine feet (2.7 m) deep. White stork nests are considered treasures in parts of Europe, where some nests have been in use for hundreds of years.

Many kinds of storks, including Abdim's, wood, and yellow-billed storks, like to nest close to one another. They are colony nesters, and a collection of nests is called a rookery. Up to several thousand pairs of storks may nest in a rookery. Other storks, including black-necked, saddle-billed, and black storks, are solitary nesters, preferring to nest away from other birds. Once a nest site has been established, storks perform a number of courtship rituals that vary by species. Some storks are quite showy. The male white stork throws his head backward, his long neck curling, until his head touches his back. Then he shakes his head to and fro. Sometimes he does this while flapping his wings. An impressed female may join in this maneuver. Other storks keep it simple. The male black stork fans his tail and bobs his head up and down. All storks make a lot of noise while courting. They clack their bills repeatedly and hiss and grunt at each other. This behavior reinforces the storks' pair bond, preparing them to share the task of raising young.

White stork nests can weigh more than 500 pounds (227 kg), sometimes causing chimneys and balconies to collapse.

Abundant elsewhere, the African openbill stork is rare in South Africa, where development has destroyed its habitat.

Stork eggs can be 4.5 inches (11.4 cm) long, or nearly twice as long as a medium-sized chicken egg.

Storks can be beneficial to farmers by eating locusts, armyworms, and other agricultural pests.

Once a year, female storks lay two to six eggs at a rate of one egg per day. A group of eggs is called a clutch. Like all birds' eggs, stork eggs must be incubated, or kept warm, while the baby storks are developing inside. Both parents take turns at gently sitting in the nest with the eggs situated under the breast and wings. Storks incubate their eggs for 28 to 37 days, after which time the baby storks, or chicks, hatch. Using its **egg tooth**, the chick chips through the hard shell of its egg. Newly hatched chicks are weak and cannot stand. Most species weigh no more than three ounces (85 g). They have only a sparse covering of fluffy feathers called down, which thickens over the next few days. The helpless chicks depend on their parents to feed them. The parents must partially digest the food they collect in order to feed the chicks. They collect food in their **crop** and carry it to the nest, where they regurgitate, or throw up, the softened mixture into the chicks' mouths.

Able to devour 60 percent of their body weight each day, the chicks grow quickly. After about three weeks, tiny feathers begin to emerge amongst the down. The chicks, now called fledglings, can stand up and flap their

Black-necked storks not only feed their young but also pour water into the chicks' mouths.

Painted storks do not develop their colorful plumage until they are between two and four years old.

scrawny wings. By the time most fledglings are about four weeks old, feathers have completely replaced their down, and they can fly. As they gain strength, young storks may leave the nest to explore their surroundings, but they will return so that their parents can continue to feed them for at least another month. At about 60 days old, the young storks leave the nest, never to return.

Many chicks do not survive even this long, though. In the Americas, tree-climbing raccoons and bobcats are the greatest predators of stork chicks, and alligators and caimans often take young birds in the water. Unguarded chicks can be plucked from their nests by birds of prey. Predatory cats such as leopards raid stork nests in Africa and Asia. Humans also play a role in chick deaths. A 2011 study by German scientists found that white stork chicks fall victim to fungal infections of the lungs, possibly caused by increased air pollution. And in 2006, **zoologists** in Poland found that litter can be deadly to chicks. More than 20 percent of the white storks studied suffered broken legs caused by entanglement in pieces of plastic that their parents had used in nest building. If they can survive their first year, most storks, such as wood storks, can live up to 18 years in the wild. Other species, such as white storks, can live 25 to 30 years. Well-fed and safe from predators, captive storks can live even longer. An oriental stork kept as part of a **captive-breeding** program in Japan died in 2007 at the age of 35. It was one of the oldest storks on record.

As people and storks are forced to share land, storks endure the consequences of human activities such as littering.

The mythical connection between storks and babies is still alive today, as shown by a 2011 storyline from Glee.

BRINGING THE BABIES

Since ancient times, the stork has been included in stories and legends. Because these birds live a long time and follow strict migration patterns, they have come to symbolize longevity in many **cultures**. In ancient Egypt, an image of a stork was used to symbolize the word *ba*, which described the spirit or personality of an object or person. The Egyptians believed the *ba* lived on even after a person died. Pictures and sculptures depicting a stork's body with a human head signified a person's *ba* leaving the body and flying toward the afterlife, where it would continue to exist forever. Storks and newborn babies were first associated with each other in ancient Greece. According to **mythology**, Gerana was a woman who did not respect the Greek gods. As punishment, the goddess Hera transformed Gerana into a stork. Missing her baby son, Mopsos, Gerana tried repeatedly to carry him away but was thwarted by her family, who did not recognize her.

The story of Gerana was retold for thousands of years, with mythical storks **evolving** into the deliverers of babies. Slavic folklore tells that the souls of unborn babies

The interior walls of the tomb of Ti, a servant of the royal Egyptian family around 2400 B.C., contain images of storks.

Grass fires draw flocks of storks, which stand on the edge of the burning grass to capture fleeing insects and other prey.

are stored in a peaceful place called Iriy, and storks go there to gather babies for delivery to expectant parents. The image of a stork flying through the air carrying a blanket-wrapped baby in its bill persists today. Mr. Stork brought Mrs. Jumbo her baby in the 1941 Disney movie *Dumbo*, and a fleet of storks delivered not only human babies but also animal babies in the 2009 Pixar short film *Partly Cloudy*. And the title characters of the 2015 Warner Bros. movie *Storks* are kept busy as well.

In 19th-century Germany, storks gained a reputation as protective good-luck charms, and flat platforms were placed on the roofs of houses to encourage storks to nest there. The Danish writer Hans Christian Andersen presented a dark side of this image in his 1838 story "The Storks." A family of storks nesting on a rooftop is cruelly taunted by a group of boys. Led by one particularly naughty boy, the group sings about the many ways to kill and roast storks. Only one good little boy refuses to join in the teasing. The stork chicks spend weeks frightened by the song. When they grow up and can fly, their mother tells them how to exact revenge on the wicked group leader. The storks fly to a magical pond where new

babies sleep underwater. They pluck two beautiful babies from the water and take them to the house of the good little boy. Having a new little brother and sister makes the boy very happy. Then the storks return to the pond and pluck out a baby that slept too long and died. They take it to the naughty boy, who learns the price of his cruelty.

Storks are prominent characters in the fables of Aesop, the legendary Greek storyteller. In one story, the frogs asked the god Zeus to send them a frog king to rule over

Storks help keep their eggs and young safe from falls by repairing and enlarging their nests each year.

THE STORK

Last night the Stork came stalking,
And, Stork, beneath your wing
Lay, lapped in dreamless slumber,
The tiniest little thing!
From Babyland, out yonder
Beside a silver sea,
You brought a priceless treasure
As gift to mine and me!

Last night my dear one listened—
And, wife, you knew the cry—
The dear old Stork has sought our home
A many times gone by!
And in your gentle bosom
I found the pretty thing
That from the realm out yonder
Our friend the Stork did bring.

Last night a babe awakened,
And, babe, how strange and new
Must seem the home and people
The Stork has brought you to;
And yet methinks you like them—
You neither stare nor weep,
But closer to my dear one
You cuddle, and you sleep!

Last night my heart grew fonder—
O happy heart of mine,
Sing of the inspirations
That round my pathway shine!
And sing your sweetest love-song
To this dear nestling wee
The Stork from 'Way-Out-Yonder
Hath brought to mine and me!

by Eugene Field (1850–95)

them. Zeus dropped a log into the frogs' pond. The big splash frightened the frogs, but soon they made fun of this thing that simply floated motionless in the water. They begged Zeus for a living ruler. Zeus then sent a stork to the pond. The stork began gobbling up the frogs. The remaining frogs hid from the stork, realizing that wishing for something new may result in something worse.

Another story features a stork that demonstrates the consequences of failing to follow the golden rule of treating others as you would like to be treated. One day, a fox decided to play a trick on the stork. He invited the stork to dinner and served a delicious fish soup in a wide, shallow bowl. While the fox eagerly lapped up the soup, the stork could do nothing more than dip the tip of his long bill into the bowl. To show the fox what a mean trick he had played, the stork invited the fox to dinner and served a scrumptious meat stew in the bottom of a tall, narrow glass. While the stork ate, the fox could lick only the drippings around the edge of the glass, which was too narrow for his face.

More than 40,000 white storks nest in Poland and are considered national treasures. A Polish folk tale explains

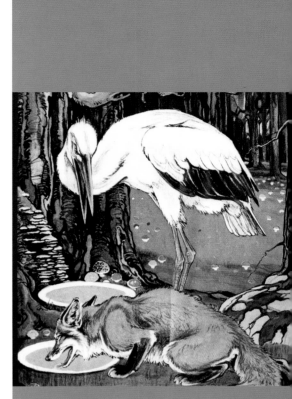

The 1921 collection of Aesop's fables was illustrated by 20th-century American artist Paul Bransom.

In 1999, the Republic of Chad included the saddle-billed stork in its series of six African bird postage stamps.

The painted stork has been seen using its wings to chase fish toward its mouth, which it holds open under water.

how storks came to be there. Long ago, God decided that frogs, lizards, and snakes had become too numerous on Earth. He put them all in a sack and then handed the sack to a human, instructing him to throw it into the abyss. But the man could not throw the sack away without first looking inside. When he opened the sack, all the creatures escaped into the marsh. God transformed the man into a stork, commanding him to find every last frog, lizard, and snake. That is why storks can be found hunting these creatures in marshes.

Postage stamps are one way that nations can celebrate important symbols. The beauty of storks hunting in their natural habitats, caring for chicks in rooftop nests, and flying across the sky has been captured in the postage stamp artwork of dozens of countries. A 2013 Lithuanian stamp honors the white stork as the country's national bird. An Algerian stamp depicts white storks flying over a mosque, and a Russian stamp shows a stork pair nesting on a rooftop that covers the globe—symbolizing the global appeal of these birds. India has released the most stork stamps, featuring oriental, white, painted, and greater adjutant storks. Australia paid tribute to the

black-necked stork, and Japan, the oriental stork. Grenada honored the wood stork, and Somalia, the marabou stork. Throughout its history, the stork has remained a revered symbol of good fortune, fertility, and family ties. Around the world, storks are considered good luck, and in many countries, killing storks or destroying their nests are actions that are not only believed to bring bad luck but are also illegal.

In addition to their regular diet of fish, painted storks have been observed catching frogs and snakes.

Once considered a member of the stork family, the shoebill is now thought to link the pelicans and storks instead.

NO ROOM FOR STORKS

All birds evolved from hollow-boned reptiles that existed millions of years ago. The link between reptiles and birds is thought to be the *Archaeopteryx*, a creature with feathered wings and reptilian teeth. It became **extinct** about 65 million years ago, but other birdlike creatures continued to evolve. Some of the oldest stork fossils in the Eastern Hemisphere date to about 30 million years ago. Fossil remains found in Egypt suggest that most prehistoric storks were about the same size and shape as modern storks. A number of similar prehistoric storks lived in Australia 30 million years ago, but the fossil remains of 2 particular species described by **paleobiologists** in 2005 were much smaller. Researchers believe that this variation allowed some storks to eat different prey, which meant the species did not compete for food. All the early storks in Australia died out, and today, only the black-necked stork remains.

Stork fossils found in the Western Hemisphere are much older and smaller than those found on the other side of the globe. In 2009, scientists from Chile discovered fossilized stork footprints on King George Island off the coast of Antarctica dating to at least 50 million years ago.

BirdLife International organizes an annual census to count white stork nests and offspring in Europe, Africa, and Asia.

Small song-birds such as sparrows and wrens build nests in the open spaces between the sticks and twigs of a stork's nest.

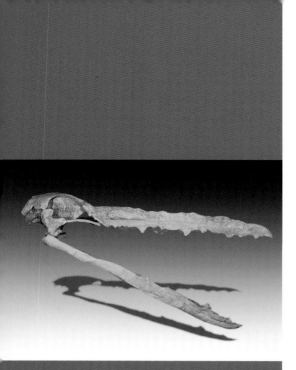

The footprints range in size from about 0.75 inch (1.9 cm) to just under 2.5 inches (6.4 cm). Historically, the storks inhabiting the Americas were believed to have evolved from Asian storks. The discovery on King George Island, however, offered evidence that New World storks may have originated in the lush tropical forests of Antarctica millions of years ago.

A very different kind of stork was discovered in 2010 on the island of Flores in Indonesia. Fossilized wing and leg fragments proved to be the remains of a marabou stork ancestor that stood 6 feet (1.8 m) tall and weighed 35 pounds (15.9 kg). Called *Leptoptilos robustus*, these birds were roughly twice the size of the people living on the island at the time—an early human-like species that stood only about 3.3 feet (1 m) tall. In 2004, **anthropologists** discovered the fossils of these people, *Homo floresiensis*, and nicknamed them hobbits. These small people shared the island of Flores with the giant storks until a major climate shift on the island drove both species to extinction about 17,000 years ago.

Although all stork species are steadily declining around the world, most species are sufficiently numerous to be listed as species of least concern by the International Union

for Conservation of Nature (IUCN). However, some species are dangerously close to extinction. Once abundant from Russia to Japan, oriental storks number fewer than 3,000 today. Destruction of wetland habitat for agriculture as well as water pollution, overfishing, and hunting drove most oriental storks out of Korea and Japan. Today, oriental storks breed in the Amur and Ussuri river basins in eastern Russia, on the border with China. The rest of the year, the storks struggle to survive in China, where they are affected by water pollution, habitat disturbance, and **poaching** for the exotic meat trade. There are restaurants in China

A Japanese captive-breeding program that started with 6 oriental storks in 1985 had more than 100 by 2007.

The Storm's stork is a solitary bird that frequents marshy lowland forests and the swampy floodplains of large rivers.

that secretly—and illegally—serve endangered animals to customers willing to pay high prices for these meals. In 2012, 33 oriental storks were poisoned in the Beidagang Wetland Nature Reserve in northern China. Workers at the Tianjin Wild Animal Rescue and Training Center were able to treat 13 of the storks and release them back into the wild, but the remaining birds died. Investigators believe poachers poisoned the birds with plans to retrieve them and sell them to a restaurant.

In Cambodia and on Malaysia's peninsula as well as on several Indonesian islands, two species of stork are in trouble. Fewer than 2,000 milky storks and only about 500 Storm's storks exist in the wild. Habitat destruction and hunting are the storks' greatest threats. About 1,600 milky and 400 Storm's storks exist on the island of Sumatra. These birds are under pressure as their forest and wetland habitats are converted to palm plantations—a practice that affects all other wildlife on the island as well. Palm oil is a valuable **commodity**, and the countries where the milky and Storm's storks live produce about 85 percent of the world's supply of palm oil.

Urbanization has driven white storks from many European countries, but they remain abundant in eastern Europe and the Middle East. Despite the storks' numbers, concerns among scientists and conservationists are mounting as more white storks are electrocuted by power lines each year. One of the first studies on this problem was conducted in Saudi Arabia in 2008. In a single month, researchers collected the bodies of 150 white storks that had been killed when they touched power lines. Storks fly high, and they build their nests in high

Because storks depend on warm air currents to push them as they migrate, they do not fly over seas or oceans.

As 1 of only 5 U.S. zoos to house maguari storks (above), the San Francisco Zoo had a maguari stork older than 35 as of 2014.

places. Nesting atop electrical towers means storks must maneuver to their nests without touching the power lines, but having long legs and wings makes that a challenge.

The wood stork was added to the United States Fish & Wildlife Service Endangered Species List in 1984, and in 2014, with rising numbers, it was reclassified as a threatened species. Habitat loss and water pollution have contributed to a major decline in wood stork populations. By the 1970s, no more than 5,000 pairs of wood storks existed in the U.S., and by 1990, fewer than 3,500 pairs existed in Mexico. However, in 2013, the U.S. government suggested removing the wood stork from the Endangered Species List because its numbers had begun to increase. Conservation efforts may have brought the wood stork back from the brink of extinction, but research conducted by the U.S. Fish & Wildlife Service found that major threats remained. A pair of wood storks needs about 440 pounds (200 kg) of food while raising a family. As urban development continues to drain or pollute wetlands, destroying storks' food supply, storks fail to successfully reproduce.

Stork conservation efforts began in the 1950s, when the National Audubon Society acquired 13,000 acres

(5,261 ha) of wetlands in southern Florida to specifically protect wood stork rookeries. The Corkscrew Swamp Sanctuary is still one of the few places in Florida where wood storks can breed undisturbed by human activities. Today, efforts are underway to reduce habitat destruction, restore wetlands, and establish protected areas for stork breeding in Georgia, South Carolina, and Florida. Storks around the world need this kind of attention if they are to survive in a world that continues to take more than storks can afford to lose.

The wood stork's featherless, dark-skinned head has earned it the nicknames "flinthead" and "ironhead."

ANIMAL TALE: STORK MAKES HYENA LAUGH

Birds have been part of African storytelling since the earliest days of human communication. Many birds are characters in pourquoi, or stories that explain how things came to be. The following tale explains the role the marabou stork played in making hyenas laugh.

Hyena has always been a crafty hunter who has never gone hungry. In fact, he is the biggest glutton in the land and always eats more than his fill. He travels where he wishes and eats what he wishes, and no one trusts him.

One day, long ago, after a satisfying meal of reedbuck, Hyena found himself in a bit of pain. A bone had become lodged in his throat. He pawed at his throat, gasping, and tried to loosen the bone, but it would not budge. "Someone must help me," he cried. But everyone was suspicious and remained hidden in the tall grass. "Come from your hiding places!" Hyena called out. "Whoever helps me will be spared from my jaws," he promised.

After some time, Pygmy Mouse crept out of the grass. "I will help you," he told Hyena, "but you must not eat me."

"I will not eat you," Hyena said. He opened his mouth, and Pygmy Mouse stepped inside. Down, down the little mouse crept until at last he came to the bone that was stuck fast in Hyena's throat. He grabbed the bone and pulled. It refused to move. He pulled harder, but still the bone did not budge. Finally, with a mighty heave, Pygmy Mouse dislodged the bone. Instantly, Hyena's mouth snapped shut, and Hyena swallowed the bone along with Pygmy Mouse. "That's much better," Hyena said.

Several weeks later, Hyena felt a familiar pain. A bone had become stuck in his throat again. "I am sorry about Pygmy Mouse," Hyena said. "I promise I will not eat whoever comes to help me. In fact," he went on, "I promise to spare your entire family."

Hyena waited a long time, gagging and vainly pawing at his throat. After some time, Gerbil came to Hyena and said, "I will help you, but you must not eat me."

"I promise," said Hyena. So Gerbil stepped inside Hyena's mouth. He found the bone and began pulling with all his might. Finally, the bone came loose. In a flash, Hyena's jaws snapped shut. Then he swallowed the bone and Gerbil in a single gulp. "I just couldn't help myself," Hyena said.

For a long time, Hyena was careful to chew the bones of his meals. However, one day as he was stuffing himself with zebra, he recklessly swallowed a bone, which became stuck in his throat. He cried out once again for help, but no one was willing to climb inside his mouth to help him.

Finally, unable to stand Hyena's bellowing any longer, Marabou Stork agreed to help. He stuck his head down Hyena's throat, and with his powerful bill, he gripped the bone and yanked it free. Instantly, Hyena's jaws snapped shut. Marabou Stork managed to pull his head out of Hyena's mouth, but all of his head feathers were left behind in Hyena's throat. This is the reason Marabou Stork has no feathers on his head and Hyena now laughs—Marabou Stork's feathers tickle his throat day and night.

GLOSSARY

anthropologists – scientists who study the history of humankind

captive-breeding – being bred and raised in a place from which escape is not possible

carrion – the rotting flesh of an animal

commodity – a raw material or agricultural product that is bought and sold

crop – a muscular pouch near the throat of some animals and birds used for food storage prior to digestion

cultures – particular groups in a society that share behaviors and characteristics that are accepted as normal by that group

DNA – deoxyribonucleic acid; a substance found in every living thing that determines the species and individual characteristics of that thing

egg tooth – a hard, toothlike tip of a young bird's beak or a young reptile's mouth, used only for breaking through its egg

evolving – gradually developing into a new form

extinct – having no living members

iridescent – showing shimmering colors that seem to change when viewed from different angles

migrating – undertaking a regular, seasonal journey from one place to another and then back again

mythology – a collection of myths, or popular, traditional beliefs or stories that explain how something came to be or that are associated with a person or object

paleobiologists – scientists who use knowledge about existing animals and their lives to answer questions about extinct animals and their lives

poaching – hunting protected species of wild animals, even though doing so is against the law

pupil – the dark, circular opening in the center of the eye through which light passes

warm-blooded – maintaining a relatively constant body temperature that is usually warmer than the surroundings

zoologists – people who study animals and their lives

SELECTED BIBLIOGRAPHY

Goodfellow, Peter. *Avian Architecture: How Birds Design, Engineer, & Build*. Princeton, N.J.: Princeton University Press, 2011.

National Geographic. "Wood Stork." http://animals .nationalgeographic.com/animals/birds/wood-stork/.

Netherton, John. *North American Wading Birds*. Stillwater, Minn.: Voyageur Press, 1998.

San Diego Zoo. "Animals: Stork." http://animals.sandiegozoo .org/animals/stork.

Smithsonian National Zoological Park. "Meet Our Animals: European White Stork." http://nationalzoo.si.edu/Animals /Birds/Facts/fact-europwhitestork.cfm.

Urfi, A. J. *The Painted Stork: Ecology and Conservation*. New York: Springer, 2011.

Note: Every effort has been made to ensure that any websites listed above were active at the time of publication. However, because of the nature of the Internet, it is impossible to guarantee that these sites will remain active indefinitely or that their contents will not be altered.

By studying changes in stork behavior, researchers can discover environmental factors that may also affect humans.

INDEX